A PAUSE
FOR POETRY

P.A.DAVIES

A PAUSE FOR POETRY

First published as a paperback in 2021 by **MJD Publishing**, 920 Hyde Road, Manchester UK.

ISBN: 9798756575637

COVER DESIGN: P.A.Davies

Please be aware that some of the poems contained within this collection contain strong language that may serve to offend certain readers. This is by no means intentional but is the subject of poetic licence.
As such, neither the author nor the publishing company will be held responsible for any offence caused to any person who reads the contents of this publication notwithstanding the warning above.

FORWARD

WELCOME one and all to this, my first book of poems. I cannot thank you enough for your support.

I first became interested in poetry many, many years ago when my grandma read to me that iconic piece from William Wordsworth:
I wandered lonely as a cloud.
I found it absolutely fascinating and to this day - some fifty years later - still hold it in great revere as my biggest influence in writing both poetry and novels.

The poems that I have selected for this book are some of my personal favorites, covering everything from the wonders of nature to the mysteries of the human mind. Indeed, some of the poems I have included were written as a mechanism to help me cope with my ongoing depression and to let others with the same affliction know that they are not - and should never be - alone.

The verses I have created are both honest and straight from the heart and I am certain that some - if not all - readers will be able to relate to a few of them in one way or another.
Above all else, I want you to enjoy reading this book as much as I have writing it.

So, with that in mind, get yourself a drink, find yourself a comfy chair and immerse yourself in a little bit of *you* time.

Afterall, we all need *a pause for poetry* at some time in our lives.

Best wishes.

Paul.

A DEDICATED POEM

I promise

How did I miss the way you felt, trapped beneath those waves of hell?
How did I miss you feeling low, a time you held desire to go?

I'm saddened that you couldn't see, a way to share your pain with me.
Nor tell me what was on your mind, when though it all, I was so blind.

And by the guilt my heart was slain, my mind tormenting me with blame.
I've never felt so broke in two, wishing I could be with you.

I feel ashamed I let you down. I feel ashamed you almost drowned.
I feel ashamed I didn't know. I feel ashamed I failed you so.

If I awoke to find you gone, no part of me could carry on.
I'd lay your picture by my side, and for the last time, close my eyes.

For life without you isn't life, so there would be no point to try.
Why live the days the way I do, when all my days I live for you?

I thank the Lord for saving you, and keeping watch whilst you pulled through.
For if he'd let the dark attend, this verse might have a different end.

But now I have a second chance, I need to look without askance.
Then bind this promise to your name: I'll never let you fall again.

Let us begin.

***

An ode to life

I eat, I drink, I sleep, I breath.

I work, I play, I cry, I grieve.

I love, I hate, I hurt, I talk.

I laugh. I joke, I run, I walk.

I like, I loathe, I give, I take.

I fear, I flee, I fight, I ache.

I look, I learn, I grow, I shout.

I pray, I trust, I fall, I doubt.

I watch, I hope, I dream. I sin.

I try, I fail, I lose, I win.

I cheer, I chant, I moan, I sigh.

An ode to life: to live, to die.

***

Remembering the '70s

I was six at the start of this decade,

by the end I was into my teens.

It's a time I remember as funky,

with lots of great years in between.

Flowery shirts with flowery ties,

a difficult mop of long hair.

Bell-bottom trousers with bright orange seams,

and tank tops of colourful glare.

Men smelling great with the great smell of Brut,

High Karate for those who were flash.

Tweed for the ladies and Yardley for Grans,

or Charlie, if short on the cash.

Jam butties with cheese, the snack of the day,

washed down with a glass of Corona.

Toffos and Spangles and Bazooka Joe gum,

Wagon wheels, the size of Verona.

I remember on Fridays, the Alpine man came,

delivering my favourite pop.

And searching the park for empty drink bottles,

cos you got ten pence back from the shop.

And fifty pence spends, if you cleaned up your room,

that could buy you a whole load of sweets.

Black Jacks and fizz bombs, a Liquorice Dip,

and a ten-penny bag full of treats.

Refreshers and Drumsticks, a choc Walnut Whip,

Curly Wurly, fruit salad and Nux.

Bar Six, Tutti Frutti, a Horror Bag snack,

and a copy of Whizzer and Chips.

Skates made of metal that strapped to your feet,

resulting in knees full of sores.

Clackers, the string that held two plastic balls,

and were finally banned by the law.

Spirograph, View Master, Dinky toy cars,

Barbie and Action man dolls.

Ludo and Cluedo and Airfix warplanes,

Scalextric, Stretch Armstrong and Trolls.

Chippers and Choppers and orange Space Hoppers,
a mullet to make you look cool.
Duffle bags, Duffle coats, a peg for your wellies,
to keep them together at school.

Sunday night baths full of blue Super Matey,
Vosene to tackle the hair.
Flannel pyjamas and blankets on beds,
to fight off the cold in the air.

Dunlop Green Flash, the rage on the streets,
to go with your new Falmer Jeans.
Lord Anthony jackets in beige corduroy,
would complete the mid-seventies dream.

Three channels were all that we had on TV,
each craving a child's allure.
With Tizwas and Swap shop and Skippy the Roo,
Basil Brush, Mister Benn and much more.

The Clangers and Playschool and Rainbow and How,
and Crackerjack showing at five,
Catch Candy, John Craven, the kids from Grange Hill,

and Runaround nnnow to survive.

A guy called Steve Austin, The Bionic Man,

each programme would give me a rush.

The Bionic woman, I have to admit,

was the source of my very first crush.

The Bay City Rollers, all Tartan and teeth,

a band that made every girl swoon.

The Osmonds, The Jacksons and Staying Alive,

and Grease with its memorable tunes.

Hide and seek, and the short three-day week,

the cold winters foggy and grey.

The longest hot summer of '76,

and a fab Butlins Camp holiday.

That time of my life was exceedingly good,

I'm glad I was actually there.

And if I could choose to keep one little part,

It would, without doubt, be the hair.

But when I look back on those glorious years,

and it may be through rosy tinted glasses,

I cannot but help feel some sadness inside,

as I think how the time quickly passes.

***

Was I wrong?

An ode to the victims of domestic violence.

Was I wrong to look the way I do?

Was I wrong the way I spoke to you?

Was I wrong the way I styled my hair?

Was I wrong to choose the clothes I wear?

Was I wrong to have a friend or two?

Was I wrong to live my life for you?

Was I wrong to give you all my love?

Was I wrong to think that was enough?

Was I wrong to laugh when you weren't there?

Was I wrong to cry in quiet despair?

Was I wrong to feel so painfully low?

Was I wrong to wish you'd let me go?

Was I wrong to loathe that first assault?

Was I wrong to think it's not my fault?

Was I wrong to trust your tearful eyes?

Was I wrong to fall for all your lies?

Was I wrong I didn't walk away?

Was I wrong to fear you every day?

Was I wrong to let you bring me down?

Was I wrong to forgive you one more time?

Was I wrong to say I'll take no more?

Was I wrong to rise up from the floor?

Was I wrong to find my inner strength?

Was I wrong to finally ask for help?

No … you were right.

***

My day in Blackpool

I walked along the prom today,

saw donkeys on the sand.

Candy floss and "kiss me quick"

and couples hand in hand.

Clowns on bikes, wax lookalikes,

and kids with bats and balls.

Horse and carts and body art,

a million donut stalls.

The wind was cold, the sun was bright,

the sea its usual grey.

And gliding down the golden mile,

the trams did make their way.

The arcades buzzed with slot machines,

a bingo caller whined.

"Two fat ladies, eighty-eight!"

One more to get a line!

The fun fare spewed the sound of screams,

and fumes of oil and sweat.

An age old game where horses race,

"Roll up and place your bets!"

The tower looms above the town,

a sight for all to see.

There's Winter gardens, skating rinks,

and yes, the Pleasure Beach.

And though my day is over now,

it took me back a while.

To family trips and happy times,

those memories make me smile

I've told you now about my day,

through the medium of rhyme.

But one more thing I have to say,

if you can spare the time?

That if, like me you class this place,

as full of crazy tack.

There's just one thing we can't deny,

Blackpool always draws us back.

Market Street (Manchester)

I sip on my coffee whilst watching the view,

of folk passing by on the street.

So, I thought I would pen you this little report,

of all of the things that I've seen.

Pram pushing mothers, a group of the brothers,

a child with a Sponge Bob balloon.

A woman that's proud to be so well endowed,

and old Alan who's strumming a tune.

There's a man in a t-shirt, displaying a sketch,

beneath it a slogan that's rude.

A busker, a beggar, a rocker in leather,

and a chick that is clearly a dude.

A bloke standing still like he's caught in a wind,

Genies that float in mid-air.

A beat boxer bops with the click of his tongue,

whilst a preacher warns all to beware.

Shoulder to shoulder with shoppers and thieves,

with no way to tell them apart.

Dodging and weaving past phone cover vendors,

and green grocers selling from carts.

Metro trams toot as they warn of approach,

pedestrians jump off the line.

The homeless look up from their old plastic cups,

and ask can you spare them a dime.

Chuggers from Oxfam start closing you down,

determined to pitch you their cause.

You smile and you lie that you're in such a rush,

and you haven't a minute to pause.

The stores overflow with those customer folk,

all aching to part with their cash.

Austerity measures? Why, what's going on?

A recession? Ha, don't make me laugh!

Loaded like camels with bags from the spree,

husbands are starting to fret.

Wives give a smile and repeat that old lie,

they've only one last thing to get.

The take-away stalls with their oniony smell,

come feast on our wares if you please?

Burgers and hot dogs and chilli with rice,

potatoes with butter or cheese.

African drummers, a guy with a harp,

some old boy dressed up as a cop.

Big issue sellers and cross-dressing fellas,

There's more to this place than just shops.

Well, that's my report on all that I've seen,

in parts quite bizarre you'll agree?

But don't take my word for it, come see yourselves,

to a place that is called Market Street.

***

Here's what I'll do

The things I will do I have put in to rhyme,

I hope that it's clear from these few random lines?

It might not seem much but it's part of a plan,

to show you my love in the best way I can.

I'll hug and I'll hold you, I'll worry, I'll cry.

I'll be totally honest yet know when you lie.

I will paint you a picture, I'll sing you a song,

I will tell you a story or say when you're wrong.

I will shout, I will play, I will spend all my money.

I will laugh at your jokes even when they're not funny.

I will guide you, advise you and tell you you can,

I will fight in your corner, 'cause that's who I am.

I will smile at your face when you're not even there.

I'll remember your voice and the smell of your hair.

I will die to protect you, will love and respect you,

'cause this was my pledge from the day I first met you.

So now that you know all the things I will do,

I'll end with this promise especially for you.

I'll always be there through the good and the bad,

For you are my life.

With love, from your Dad. xxx

***

Me at Fifty

I looked in the mirror and what did I see?

Some half-century bloke staring right back at me.

I prodded and poked at the deep laughter lines,

I checked out the grey and then uttered a sigh.

Who is this stranger and where have I gone?

That cannot be me, cos I feel twenty-one.

I'm down with the kids and I'm hip to the core,

I'm not that old man who just looks like a bore.

I can still party hard and I know how to rock.

I can still strut my stuff, almost past ten o'clock.

My clothes are quite trendy, I'm still looking SIC,

I can still LMAO when texting the chicks.

I blog and I post and I hashtag the trend,

I like and I follow the status of friends.

Facebook and Twitter and candy crush three,

I'm cool and I'm hip ... so whatsapp with me?

Well:

Maybe it's time to face up to the truth,

I'm fifty years old and no longer a youth.

I don't paint the town red nor fall out of pubs,

hell, I visit the Doctors more times than the clubs.

And that noise in my ears, or so people say,

is Key 103 with the hits of today.

What happened to music and why's it so bad?

Oh, heavens above, now I sound like my dad.

Okay, I concede, raise my hands in the air,

I need reading glasses. I'm losing my hair.

I nap on the couch more than ever before,

I've taken a liking to Radio four.

And so what?

Here's to being fifty, happy birthday to Paul.

I'm blessed to be here and still having a ball.

There's not much I'd change in the life that I've led,

so, let's raise a glass to the future instead.

And that man in the mirror who's staring at me,

not looking as taut as I'd like him to be.

Here's to you friend and the life yet to come,

Wear a smile on your face cos you ain't fifty-one.

Yet!

***

An ode to war

Nations rise and go to war,

to settle all their ancient scores.

O'er religion, land and oil and greed,

Whilst in their young, they plant the seed.

That talk is cheap with no reward.

The pen is not the mighty sword.

And only those who stand and fight,

who face their fears and earn the right,

shall have a voice that all will hear,

and prosper on the battlefield.

And so the youth take up their plight,

too young to know for what they fight.

Eyes that say their souls are dead,

once laughing hearts now beat with dread.

And happy times have been dismissed,

their names fill up the reaper's list.

No more a time for song or dance,

the hope to live, their only chant.

Lords of War will fill the troughs,

with Dirty Bombs, Kalashnikovs,

and serve up cold, to those who wait,

their weapons made for savage hate.

They will not care the flow of blood,

that runs from all the murdered good.

For missiles, mines and antitanks,

mean dollars bulge in swollen banks!

Let's pray that God will show his face,

and smile upon the human race.

Then call upon his fellow man,

to stop the deaths the best they can.

But though the answer is quite clear,

not everyone will want to hear.

That age-old line they've heard before.

Give peace a chance, we've had our wars.

***

The Wind

Today the wind is quiet

Not speaking, nor whispering.

Yet it waits.

It waits and it watches, not speaking, nor whispering.

Soon it will waken and reach.

With a groan and a hiss it will reach.

And it will speak.

But not today.

Today it is quiet.

Have I heard it?

Yes. It has spoken to me.

It called and it cried and then it howled, as if …

As if it were angry, annoyed that I might not listen.

But I listened.

And I felt and I witnessed.

Felt its icy grasp around my bones, punishing them.

Witnessed it take the shine from the moon as it threw battered clouds across

her face.

And I was held, with no escape.

I have seen trees bend as if in worship to it,

Seen man and beast alike, run from it,

Hoping – praying – that its anger would cease.

But …

Today the wind is quiet.

Not speaking nor whispering.

But it will come my friend.

It will come!

***

Memories Of You

You are my fondest memories.

Sweet like the smell of a new spring day.

Like the crystal glisten of dew in the sunlight of dawn, how your beauty

sparkled.

To me these things were you.

When we touched, sensations of joy pulsated through my every nerve.

Passion from deep within me stirred and came to life, like a darkened sky

made bright by the silvery beams of a rising moon.

Like a warm summer breeze, how gentle you breathed.

Like a tranquil pool of green, how your eyes invited me in.

And from within a perfect frame of red, your smile would melt away the

icicles of troubles from around my heart.

Oh yes, you are my fondest memories.

***

The Salesman

Good day Sir, can I help you?

Or are you looking round?

This one is all the rage right now.

It's only ninety pounds.

May I make one suggestion?

I feel that's much too small.

I think Sir should try this one.

Too bright? Why not at all.

Or maybe Sir likes this one?

It also comes in blue.

Oh marvellous, marvellous choice Sir,

I'll have it wrapped for you.

And how will Sir make payment?

By bank cheque, cash or card?

Oh, that will do quite nicely.

Thank you, Sir … yes, goodbye.

You know Gerard it's funny,

quite startling, when you think.

That a "Lord" like he, would want to wear,

a dress in shocking pink.

***

The life & times of a Television

I was sitting with my friends one day,

all warm and quite content,

when salesman Dave, all teeth and spots, said,

"Here's the one to rent!"

Then Mister Jones, his wife and kids,

came up to take a view.

They fiddled, pulled and twisted knobs,

I knew my days were few.

I said goodbye to all my friends,

a teardrop in my eye,

and hoped that Dave, all grease and suit,

forgot to mention Sky.

Jones' took me home and plugged me in,

on view for all to see.

They flicked around from 2 to 4,

from 1 and then to 3.

They fiddled with my aerial,

turned the volume up and down.

Watched National News, a thousand soaps,

and moved me round and round.

And finally came the VCR,

and a year of BSB.

When in the end, I blew my tubes;

It was all too much for me.

So now I sit in Jim's Repairs,

on sale for twenty quid.

I only hope the next to buy,

Won't treat me like Jones' did.

***

Visions of a Sinner

Hell opened its fiery gates and I stood before Death.

Familiar voices beckoned, commanding me to enter but I dared not, for I

knew it was eternal.

I sought a way to leave, to return to what was before but all those roads

were gone, no passage remained.

I wept and was afraid yet moved towards the clutches of doom knowingly,

but not of my own will.

I was drawn in, powerless to resist.

I called for help but comfort was not at hand.

And why should it be?

I was alone to meet my fate.

Destiny had arrived.

***

Thunderstorm

"Rain, rain, go away!"

I've heard so many people say.

But malice clouds that won't be told,

do spit at us a liquid cold.

As thunder roars and lightning strikes,

the darkest skies do come alight.

And heaven throws its sodden darts,

to drench our bones and chill our hearts.

The rivers swell, the houses shake,

whilst age-old trees do bend and break.

And I have seen the great oaks fall,

when bitten by the Devil's fork.

Another flash of blinding light,

makes silhouettes against the night.

And then, as if the sky were torn,

the thunder makes an angry groan.

And children weep and hide in fear,

afraid that demons will appear.

For on these nights, they have been told,

the Bogeyman will claim their souls.

When at last its work is done,

and prayers have helped the best they can.

The angry beast will move away,

but lie in wait for other days.

***

The beatitudes of literature

If Jesus gave his sermon

upon that mount today,

he'd preach a love of literature,

and this is what he'd say.

Blessed are the Authors,

who inspire, surprise, delight.

Blessed are the bookworms,

who read into the night.

Blessed are the bloggers,

who spread the news to all,

and tell us what is good or bad,

which books may rise or fall.

Blessed are the book shops,

that stock their shelves with art.

Blessed are the ardent fans,

so loyal in their hearts.

Blessed are the scholars,

for writing skills they teach.

That helped to bring us all the greats,

like Shakespeare, Dickens, Keats.

Blessed are the libraries,

each filled with books galore.

From volumes full of knowledge,

to fiction, fact and more.

And blessed be the audiotape,

from text to spoken word.

The blind, and those not keen to read,

can hear a whole new world.

Now please, don't think me blasphemous,

or view me down your nose.

I write without impiety,

and humble in my prose.

But ... here's the thing.

I'm privileged to be on this earth,

amongst great raconteurs.

Who share their gift with all of us,

in chapter, song and verse.

So let us praise the writers,

who fill our hearts and souls,

with words of glee or tales of woe;

Our Father ... bless them all.

Amen.

***

Me, Myself and I

I watch the days pass by me,

they flash before my eyes.

So many things to test me,

lows, without the highs.

I feel myself imploding,

I feel I cannot breathe.

I feel my mind is closing ranks,

I feel my good thoughts leave.

I want to sleep a thousand years,

I want to run a mile.

I want much more than disaccord,

I want to keep my smile.

I need to wake up daily,

knowing I'll be fine.

I need to share my feelings,

but all I do is hide

I have to stop believing,

that this is here to stay.

I have to start believing,

today's a brighter day

I know I'm not the only one,

an island on my own.

I know that others feel this way,

lost and so alone.

But maybe they are hiding?

Or is it that I'm blind?

For though I look, I only see,

what's lurking in my mind.

This morning there is sunshine,

a blue and cloudless sky.

It might just be a better day,

for me, myself and I.

***

Lost

It's hard to tell you how I feel,

I can't explain, it seems unreal.

When pieces wander from my mind,

and leave those empty gaps behind.

I cannot tell you where I went,

but please don't think me ignorant.

Deaf to what you have to say,

muted, blind, so far away.

Those thieves of thought don't seem to care,

they take my mind from here to there.

Fill my heart with angst and fear,

then send me back when I feel tears,

track unannounced along my face,

to wash me back from empty space.

It's like …

It's like the wires, inside my brain,

burn out and blow a fuse again.

Pull me down and make me low,

I feel I have no place to go,

but deep into my own recourse,

to try and rectify the cause.

Yet even I don't understand,

how suddenly I'm half the man.

So different to the former me,

living life through comedy.

Who tried to brighten other's gloom,

ironic how they've left the room,

now that I need a helping hand,

someone to hear, to understand.

Mind you ...

I don't expect that they have seen,

the darkest places I have been.

But should they fear what they can't see?

Not knowing what to say to me?

Staring with those judging eyes,

hoping, praying, I'll walk by.

I haven't got a dread disease.

You cannot catch my misery.

You will not make my symptoms worse,

engaging me in simple verse.

I'm not okay but that's okay,

I'll make it through another day.

I'm taking every step I can,

to make myself a normal man.

Whatever normal is?

I ask for patience from you all,

to give me time to reach my goal.

I won't be fixed within a week,

not even with the help I seek.

But here's the thing that matters most,

I still have life that's left to toast.

So, fight I must and fight I will,

I'll win the fight, I won't give in.

I'll find a way to help unblock.

I'll find a key to help unlock.

And find I will, with fingers crossed,

a mind that ... well, for now ... is lost.

***

The Critic with a heart

I had a book which only took,

a day for me to read.

I must confess, I'm self-obsessed,

with finishing at speed.

And of this book, which only took,

a day for me to drain.

I thought the prose was mighty close,

to driving me insane.

It had no plot and lacked a lot,

of structure to its text.

I cannot start to call it art,

it really got me vexed.

The title sucked, I wasn't hooked,

by badly written blurb.

The cover pic just made me sick,

its concept quite absurd.

But being me, I hate to see,

my critique seeming sore.

I'll hold my tongue and play along,

and join the book's blog tour.

I'll say it's cool, despite the fool,

who thinks that he can write.

And once again I'll recommend,

when honestly? It's shite.

Opinions count, but casting doubt,

can ruin an author's head.

"I can't believe you cannot see, the best thing since sliced bread!"

Some might say.

So, I will do a fair review,

but never go too far.

Yet books I hate - I'll tell you straight –

will only get one stars .... maybe two.

Anyway.

As now's the time to end this rhyme,

I'll close with this impart.

I cannot do a bad review,

it's not within my heart.

That's somewhat tame and kind of lame,

I hear the readers call.

But best to rate a book not great,

than rate no books at all.

***

My Friends

Lift me up when I fall down.

Catch me if I start to drown.

Find a ray of hope to send.

Where would I be without my friends?

Days when I am feeling low.

Sliding down as bad thoughts grow.

Grip the bleak and make it end.

Where would I be without my friends?

See the darkness, taste the rain.

The sun's gone down inside my brain.

Make the light shine, ease my pend.

Where would I be without my friends?

Behold my saviours, look and see.

Twenty milli-grams a piece.

Bring me back, repair the seams.

These friends I call Fluoxetine

Yet to the future I must look.

Reclaim the soul my demons took.

Looking forward, life to wend.

Time to breathe, to make amends.

Fight a fight worth fighting for.

Eradicate and settle scores.

See the light, the tunnel's end.

No more the need to use my friends?

Hopefully.

***

Some Days

It feels like I've fallen through ice on a lake,

Black, gelid water, no chance of escape.

Desperate to breathe, not seeing the light.

Praying to God that I'll be all right.

Some days I'm elated to be in my shoes,

laughing and hopeful, no cancerous gloom,

to catch me again with its unannounced sleight.

These are the days I'm not under the ice.

Some days my process of thought isn't right,

wandering or distant or unwilling to fight,

for that spark of belief when belief's all it takes,

to stop me from falling once more in the lake.

Some days I dwell on the Grim Reaper's goal,

and when might he visit to drain out my soul,

from the life that I have, from the life that I lead?

Will I be sleeping? Will I be freed?

Will I know when it happens?

Will I fill with remorse?

Will I stand before God?

Will I have some recourse,

to claim back my being and grab for the line,

that'll save me from sinking, from losing my mind?

Some days - in some ways - I feel out of place,

Though you'll never guess from the look on my face,

how some days - in most ways - I'm drowning inside,

and biting my tongue for the sake of my pride.

But one day I know that this sorrow and pain,

will fade like a breath on a cold window pane.

My mind won't be troubled by flashes of doom.

One day, someday, hopefully soon.

***

M People

Beyond the glass I'm looking through,

people scurry back and to.

Soldier ants that march in line,

stop for nothing, spare no time.

Ears plugged, iPods, mobile phones.

Circumscribed, recessive clones.

Human vehicles, rolling roads.

Auto pilots, cruise control.

Hurry here and make haste there,

straining from the cross they bear.

Sullen faces hide their best,

eyes to footpath, chin to chest.

Manchester People, spare some time.

Listen to what I have in mind.

It's free advice, there is no "sell".

It's just a thought on which to dwell.

Put the brakes on, slow your pace,

it's only called "the human race".

Take a moment, make a pledge,

change the path you always tread.

Smile at someone passing by.

Lift your head up, face the sky.

Feel the sunshine, taste the rain.

Take a breath and breathe again.

Laugh out loud so people stare.

Dance as though you just don't care.

Sit and watch the world go by.

Make the most of this, your time.

Become the piper, set the beat.

Be a shepherd not a sheep.

Step back, hold back, think stuff through.

Prioritise the things you do.

Don't fear trying, don't fear change.

Don't fear failing, try again.

Don't waste time with times of strife.

Above all else, don't waste your life.

So, lift your heads up city folk.

Cast aside your personal yolks.

Embrace your lot, be proud to say;

"I took that breath, I breathed again!"

***

The meaning of life

According to me

When you analyse the reason,

when you sit and think it through,

our lives have much more meaning,

than what we all assume.

It's not about the job, the house,

the brand-new fancy car.

It's not about possessions nor

how smartly dressed we are.

It's not our grades from school that count.

It's not about promotion.

It's not a stage for hate or greed,

or craving some devotion.

Look around and you will see,

a world that's so enchanted.

Tightly packed with Nature's gifts,

we often take for granted.

Flowers, sunshine, hills of green,

seasons of the year.

Rain and snow and wind and ice,

waters crystal clear.

Mountains, rainbows, waterfalls,

wildlife big and small.

Forests, deserts, polar caps,

let's wonder at them all.

Barefoot in a meadow,

through golden fields of corn.

Diamonds made from morning dew.

Weathering a storm.

People laughing, babies born,

trees with Autumn hues.

Starlit skies and thunder clouds,

oceans glistening blue.

Embrace this day as though your last,

behold the Earth you're on.

Tomorrow isn't guaranteed,

and yesterday has gone.

Touch it, see it, breathe the air,

a privilege, not a right.

Reach beyond your safe cocoon,

explore what's out of sight.

Leave your mark, a legacy,

a story to remember.

So when it's time to meet your God,

you'll be more than a memory.

But remember ...

It isn't just the visual,

that makes a life run true.

We need to tweak the actual,

the things we say and do.

It's sharing, caring, spreading love.

Of joy we need to tell.

Respecting other people,

who walk this world as well.

Degrees are not the things you need,

to help your fellow man.

It doesn't take a millionaire,

to lend a helping hand.

A random act of kindness.

One selfless deed a day.

Helping those less fortunate,

to find another way.

And finally ...

To end this ode I wish to close,

with words from a famous bat.

To those of you that heed these words,

I warmly tip my hat.

"It's not who you are but what you do that defines you!"

La fin.

****

Like. Comment. Share.

An ode to social media

Open my laptop and what do I see?

People are sharing their whole lives with me.

Requests to be friends with a friend of my boss,

random narration of fortune or loss.

Look at my dog, with a bow tie and hat.

Look at the antics of my crazy cat.

Look at this burger I'm hoping to eat.

Look at the snow that just fell on our street.

Drool o'er my pint, whilst I sit in this bar.

Watch how I lip sync whilst driving my car.

Feel all my suffering or bask in my glee.

Look at my baby who's just turning three.

Look at my knees whilst I lie in the sun,

pinned on a map where I'm checking in from.

Update and comment, like, love or hate,

try to delete when you know it's too late.

Proffer opinion or share someone's thought.

Post dissertations or just keep it short.

Update your status' five times a day.

Look at my pride cos I ran the 10k.

Post from your armchair on series' well known,

Love island, X-factor, the new Game of Thrones.

Holidays, birthdays, weddings and more,

invites to pages you've not seen before.

But ... wait a minute.

Is this the life we are destined to lead,

eye strain from staring too long at our screens?

Vocal chords silenced, replaced with a text,

thumbs with no skin on and cricks in our necks?

Let's take a moment to dwell on our roots,

the days before smartphones controlled what we do.

The times when a friend was a person you knew.

The times when a "like" didn't mean much to you.

And I say this ...

Though social media is destined to stay,

I want to remind you to live for the day.

Have an adventure away from your screen,

look at the world and then go find your dream.

For life can't be lived through the touch of an app.

A chat room's no place for an actual chat.

So, get up and go out if just for a while.

Marvel at nature to bring on a smile.

And now, to conclude, I would just like to say,

that all social media is fine as a play.

Just don't let the network take over your head,

for there's no second chance when you status reads ... "dead".

***

The Impartation

I once met a fella,

an old storyteller,

who told me the key to success.

He breathed in my ear,

so that no one would hear,

the secret that he did possess.

And when he was done,

it felt like the sun,

was lighting up all of my mind.

"Be fearless," he said.

"Leave nothing unsaid,

be loyal, be honest, be kind."

"Be true to yourself - but above all else - remember to follow your heart."

And with that he smiled,

through eyes that beguiled,

and left without further impart.

I willed his return, but by showing concern,

he had done what he needed to do.

So, I let him go, but hopefully so,

I will see him again someday soon.

I opened my eyes,

and to my great surprise,

I didn't feel solemn or sad.

And whether a dream or vision I'd seen,

I will cherish the words of my dad.

***

The Disingenuous Ones

Sly like foxes, thick as thieves,

lay upon their cardboard sleeves.

Handwritten signs that swear to all,

they don't do drugs or alcohol.

With doleful eyes and tales of woe,

they bleed the good from decent folk.

Loiter by the cash machines,

intimidate by silent means.

Shake a cup, ask for change,

nod then fall asleep again.

Blankets they will never fold.

Sleeping bags to fight the cold.

Backs against a rubbish bin.

"This is my space, don't step in!"

Hierarchical begging zones,

angry stares and bitter tones.

Rotting teeth and shaking bones,

courtesy of methadone.

Cans of lager, Diamond White.

Piss and spit and drunken fights.

But don't be fooled by what you see,

they don't all live in misery.

For many travel from their homes,

and sit upon these streets of gold,

to feign a life without device,

that reaps the coin that buys the spice.

Then scurry off to find their thrill,

a gift for which you've paid the bill.

So now I call upon the Mayor,

to show us that he really cares,

by pledging help for those in need,

and rid us of those fuelled by greed.

Sir.

The truly homeless need support,

compassion, hope, a kindly thought.

Not treating with the same distaste as those that now infest the place.

Look around your City streets,

see the ones that lie and cheat.

Address the problem, clean the mess.

Let's stop the disingenuous.

Yours sincerely.

A resident.

***

Springtime

This morning I opened my curtains,

and felt such a warmth in my heart.

For blue sky and sunshine did greet me again,

Springtime's beginning to start.

My daffodil heads are unfolding,

my tulips are looking the part.

My spirits are lifted this wonderful day,

as springtime's beginning to start.

I see children playing, hear lawnmowers whirr,

whilst families descend on the park.

Hand in hand lovers just happy to stroll,

when Springtime's beginning to start.

Wood pigeons calling, blackbirds in song,

a fanfare to Nature's New Year.

So love and live it and breathe in the air,

for springtime is finally here.

***

#amwriting

Stories of love, of mystery, of fun,

some that will end up quite tragic.

Words that are sent by the Literary Gods,

to store in my head full of magic.

Heroes and Villains all biding their time,

to anger, surprise or delight.

Plots that will leave you suspended in time,

gripped whilst you read through the night.

I'll master my craft in the hope you'll embrace,

the words that I scribe on a page.

For a good book should court you, beguile and transport you,

regardless of gender or age.

I thank you for caring, supporting and sharing,

hashtag amwriting for you.

I gift you this rhyme and will end with the line,

of a quote that I hold to be true.

"In a world full of imagination, anything is possible!"

Through my eyes

A marbled mix of grey and green,

oh, what sights my eyes have seen.

Cataloguing years gone by,

photos stored within my mind.

And through this gift I came to learn,

the pulchritude of this fine Earth.

Rainbow prisms in the sky,

snow-capped mountains stretching high.

Summer sunshine, pouring rain,

flowers bloom with life again.

Like a blanket, night unfurls,

revealing stars that shroud our world.

Babies born and Blackbirds sing,

a plethora of wondrous things.

But with this gift, I've also seen,

what lurks beyond these pleasantries.

The greed of man akin to beast,

third world famine, western feast.

Senseless wars and needless crime,

people wasting precious time.

Hatred flows, an unstemmed bleed,

wounds of colour, sex or creed.

Pain when pain is not the way,

turn our backs, discriminate.

So let us stop and think things through.

Change our paths, try something new.

Look at life with open eyes,

the answer's simple if we try.

Love our friends, embrace our foes.

Come together, share the load.

Stop the killing, find a cure.

In Lennon's words, "Make love not war".

A marbled mix of grey and green,

so many sights my eyes have seen.

I hope one day ALL eyes will see,

A world of joy, a world of peace.

When Sunday was Sunday

The shops were all shuttered, with "Closed" on the doors.

A typical Sunday before we craved more.

Roads without traffic, stores without lines.

Lie ins, late breakfasts and family time.

Stay in pyjamas and crash on the couch.

Throw on some wellies to take the dog out.

Dads' sponge the cars down; Mums' roast the meat.

Church for believers, who pray for the meek.

No consoles to play on, no smartphones to use.

No Twitter, no Facebook, no Instagram news.

Friends at your back door, to go and play out.

True social circles without any doubt.

Riding a chopper bike, building a den.

No Xbox 360 or YouTube back then.

Sunday league football and kids in the park.

Tend the allotment until it went dark.

Nothing on TV before "Songs of Praise"

So, let's play Monopoly, then watch "Howard's Way" … [Google it]

When home cooked roast dinners took many an hour,

cos Beefeaters were people that guarded a tower.

No TFI Fridays to carry the load,

no fancy-pant carveries that charge through the nose.

Some say that Sundays were boring and grey,

a prequel to working the very next day.

But my view is simple, I feel we were blessed.

When Sunday was Sunday:

a day full of rest.

***

The Diminishing Blue Line

Dedicated to all frontline police officers around the world

Twenty plus years I had a career,

of putting my life on the line.

Flying the flag on behalf of the service,

Whilst sorting the next nine-nine-nine.

Eager to right and ready to fight,

in spite of unfavourable odds.

Give marriage guidance to keep the Queen's peace,

between the same families of yobs.

Spat on and shat on with little respect,

the public increases demand.

Spat on and shat on with sod all succour,

from those up above in command.

No time for welfare, just jobs in a queue,

Officers sent single crewed.

Grade one domestics or fights breaking out,

a cop has no option to choose.

Our rest days get cancelled, our breaks get cut short,

our pensions illegally changed.

Substandard equipment has little effect,

when fighting with fools on cocaine.

We took on the chin that our numbers were thin,

yet still kept the wheel on each day.

But now where we stand - and throughout the land -

that iconic blue line fades away.

If bitter I'm sounding, then bitter I am,

your protectors are down on their knees.

Pleading with Government to do something more,

but they just ignore all our pleas.

Our Fed says it fights to enforce basic rights,

of officers stuck in this farce.

They promise a win but fall for the spin,

when the Home Office shafts their weak arse.

Oh, but here's a free pen colleagues!

A service we are and PC we must be,

transparent despite the effects.

We've opened the gates and now it's too late.

We've lost all belief and respect.

It's becoming inherent that arrest's no deterrent,

when offenders get slapped on the wrist.

Enforcing the law seems appropriate no more,

as it's all about setting them free.

Example A.

Offender demands a most stern reprimand,

for an officer doing his job.

"Cos the Taser he used made my skin red and bruised, and right now I can't

feel ma nob!"

Aw.

*Boo - f**king - hoo!*

However:

Complaint Upheld. Officer disciplined.

Offender - released without charge - went on to stab his partner!

Justice?

The rights of the racist, the robber, the rapist,

are something you daren't compromise.

Yet help for the victims - who suffer the traumas –

is rapidly on the demise.

As for me?

Well:

I've broken my bones, been kicked in the nose,

been shot at and threatened with knives.

My spine is all twisted,

my health not so good.

I'm thinking a cat has less lives

Though hard to report, I asked for support,

to cope with my PTSD.

I held a belief that the "family" still cared,

how wrong could an officer be?

And so.

Battered and bruised, deflated, abused,

with no more the will to fight on.

I look to the time, just a few days away,

When I can say "See ya, I'm gone!"

But let me just end with this footnote my friends,

by saying it's not all been coarse.

Those days way back when,

I would do them again.

If they'd let us police as a force.

If only.

***

With love from

You hold me without even touching my skin.

Your eyes so hypnotic they're drawing me in.

Your smile so enchanting,

your humour a craft.

The way that your hair falls,

the way that you laugh.

Into my arms, place your head on my chest.

Hear my heart beating,

no longer bereft.

Filled with the warmth of the joy that you bring.

I'd sing you a love song,

if o' I could sing.

Lying beside me, you whisper my name.

You say that you love me, I mirror the same.

Interlocked fingers, baring our souls.

Two halves of love now becoming a whole.

The wondrous stars of a dark cloudless night.

The rise of the sun showing nature's delights.

These things I know are amazing and true,

but nothing compares to the beauty of you.

So here is a promise I need you to hear.

I'll share my emotions without any fear.

For you, I will be all the best that I can.

I'm here for you always.

With love from your man.

***

Moving forward, glancing back

A New Year's poem

I've seen good people struggle,

I've watched my close one's cry.

I myself have fought a fight,

with shadows in my mind.

I've seen the birth of babies,

a generation new.

I've prayed that God will keep them safe;

the least that he can do.

I've listened to the joy of friends,

embraced their misery.

I've tried the very best I can,

to be a better me.

I've laughed so hard my body ached,

I've cried a thousand tears.

I've dreamt a life worth living for,

despite my hidden fears.

I've dwelled on things that could have been,

decisions in my past.

Choices made or chances lost,

the year has gone so fast.

I'm moving forward carefully,

whilst glancing back in time.

Holding on to memories,

that help me walk the line.

And now that time has come again,

when promises are made.

Auld Lang Syne, bring in the new,

for this is New Year's Day.

May your year be filled with joy,

where good outweighs the bad.

May the health of you and yours,

be the best you've ever had.

But please...

Remember there are folk out there,

whose lives are not so blessed.

The ones who yearn for basic needs:

so, here's what I suggest.

Spare a thought or say a prayer,

help them if you can.

It needn't be spectacular,

there needn't be a plan.

The smallest thing can mean so much,

to those we all forsake.

One random act of kindness,

is all it really takes.

Thank you.

Happy New Year

***

No time

I have no time to think of me,

I have no time at all.

It seems that when I try to think,

I answer someone's call.

There are no minutes left for me,

to give a little thought,

to all those puzzles in my head,

I really need to sort.

I have no time to sit and dwell,

to catch myself and breathe.

I cannot analyse my mind,

although it's what I need.

I find no space reserved for me,

but should I really care?

Cos truth be told and truth be heard,

my troubles don't compare;

with what's bestowed to those on Earth,

less fortunate than me,

so, who am I to shed a tear,

because I fail to see?

That if, by chance, a moment comes,

in which I can reflect,

it'll take no more a heartbeat,

to realise I'm blessed.

***

The Tree of Life

Come stand before the Tree of Life,

to banish all your woeful strife.

For from its roots connection flows

to breathe new strength into the soul.

I sense a growth of kismet here,

a way to quell my inner fears.

A warm uniqueness in its calm,

that shelters me from boding harm.

Branches reaching far and wide,

bearing fruit for all to try.

A rebirth of the heart and mind,

a place of peace for all mankind.

There's no discrimination here,

no prejudice, no need for fear.

Come black or white, come rich or poor,

the Tree of Life embraces all.

It welcomes you as family,

lends you sight that you may see,

another path, a better way,

to leave the past and live today.

So, sit beneath this canopy,

a sanctum of tranquillity.

Until you see that guiding light,

come shining through your Tree of Life.

***

This Town

These broken streets around my home,

I once was proud to call my own,

have now become so worn and grey.

This town has seen much better days.

Buildings new surround the old,

we watch the modern landscape grow.

A true depiction of our times?

Just look below those building lines.

Pavements strewn with putrid mess,

filled with so called homelessness.

Intimidating groups decree,

"I need your change to fill my needs."

Shouting, swearing, spitting swine;

they won't get a council fine.

Debris dumped upon the ground;

it's looking like a shanti town.

I know that some may snub this rhyme,

suggest I'm cruel and that is fine.

But blinkered views won't cure this kink,

I only write what others think.

We've watched this epidemic grow,

a product of the seeds we've sown.

Addicts playing homeless games,

when most have homes yet feel no shame.

They steal the hope of honest men,

those whose plight is genuine.

And pray upon the weak and kind:

we need to stop it, draw a line.

In earnest we must stand before,

all those who preached intent to cure,

the rot that's spreading like disease,

and ask how long they plan to leave,

this wretched growth within our town,

that's set to bring our spirits down?

Manchester, upon your throne,

I've loved you like you were my own.

But sadness lurks to bring me down

If we can't save my home, this town.

Let's try.

***

Change

There's not a lot I ask of life,

I'm not a man of greed.

A smiling face, a warm embrace,

will satisfy my needs.

I do not crave a fancy car,

I do not yearn for fame.

Yet though I pray for health and peace,

I've not always been the same.

I once believed the key to life,

was based on what you earn.

That money was the only goal,

but thankfully I've learnt.

It's not about the paths of gold,

that many seek to find,

as searching for elusive wealth,

can push your life aside.

Your family and your closet friends,

the food upon your plate.

These are worth a whole lot more,

than any deal you'll make.

So, changing just the smallest thing,

to brighten up your day,

would be a step to better times;

a less destructive way.

Now take a moment, think a while,

and search within your soul.

Then ask yourself if what you do,

is really worth it all.

Or could you take a different route,

to lighten up your load?

Believe me when I say to you,

there is no finer road.

Work to live, not live to work,

a quote I took from Noel.

But work to live a life that's full,

let living be your goal.

So, raise the sails and set your course,

go ride across the waves.

And leave those "what-ifs" on the shore.

It's time to seize your day.

***

Protest

Why can't people have their say

and come together for a day,

without the fools who's only thought,

is bragging on the cops they've fought.

Why can't people air their views

without the actions of a few,

claiming to be part of change,

when violence is their only aim.

Why can't people speak their minds,

and pave a way for better times,

without the groups of mindless thugs - intent on marring all that's good –

skulking with the peaceful souls,

when peace will never be their goal.

Freedom, change, equality,

the right to who you want to be.

Things that should be set in stone,

without the need to fill the roads.

Black lives matter, that is true,

but I say ALL lives matter too.

We need to come together whole,

eradicate the pain and woes,

of those that need our help the most.

Let love and caring be our boast.

Not tweeting who did this or that.

Not rising to the media crap.

Not spoiling for a brutal fight.

Not judging every cop in sight.

No heavy-handed crowd control.

No bitter words nor tainted soul.

No thinking 'you are less than me'.

No 'them and us' mentality.

I hope my words are loud and clear,

so you can see the message here?

To harvest change by planting seeds,

a peaceful protest's all it needs.

***

Do you?

When you hear all the echoes of silence,

and there's nothing but darkness within.

When the weight of the world seems eternally yours,

do you think that it's time to give in?

When it feels like you've lost all your passion,

in a maze full of shadow and doubt.

When your reasoning wanes and your sanity frays,

do you lose faith to figure it out?

When life only seems an uncountable noun,

and adjectives mould a dark view.

Of meaningless, pointless and desperate thoughts,

do you dwell on the wrong thing to do?

But think…

Will the world keep on spinning without you?

Will the plight of the needy be cured?

Will anything change bar eventuate grief?

Tell me now; do you care anymore?

Do you fight?

Do you cry?

Do you scream?

Do you try, to put all the pieces in place?

Does the future seem bleak?

Do you feel that you're weak?

When you can't put a smile on your face.

Those days when you feel you are broken?

Those times you're consumed by the blue?

Don't feel you're alone.

You're not on your own.

For these are the things I feel too.

So, try this.

Call upon all of your memories.

The ones that were cast from your joy.

Chase them, embrace them and take back the light.

Then show all your demons the door.

Recount all the days of your happy.

Banish those chains of dismay.

Breakout and reach out, then shout out with might...

"It's okay not to be so okay!"

***

Blinded

There are times in our lives when we seem to lose sight,

of things that are making us whole.

We tend to forget and then drown in regret,

as the happiness bleeds from our souls.

It makes little sense to be sat on the fence,

when it comes to affairs of the heart.

Yet often the fool who is playing it cool,

will see their whole world tear apart.

Set in your ways can evoke darker days,

it's time to embrace changing times.

No two are the same and love's not a game,

so please don't relate to this rhyme.

For these are the words that are quite often heard,

from those that have thrown it away.

Blinded from reason and things that have meaning.

The grass is not greener, I say.

If gratitude's dormant then please take a moment,

remember what first caused that shine.

Don't be ashamed to relive it again,

For love should have no finish line.

So finally I say, let this be a new day.

Start as you mean to go on.

Cherish those things that are making you whole,

and treat them as second to none.

***

Wish

I used to wish upon a star,

not knowing it was way too far,

to hear the things I had to say,

yet still I'd wish most every day.

I'd wish for it to stop the rain,

and let the sun shine through again.

But maybe through that thick grey cloud,

it couldn't hear me wish out loud.

I'd wish a life of being grand,

or touring with my teenage band.

An actor on the stage I'd be,

if that bright star had noticed me.

I'd wish for courage, wish for strength,

to finally kiss the girl I'd met.

Wish for summer, wish for snow,

wish my days in school weren't slow.

Oh, the wishes of the young.

These days I've no request for wealth,

no wish for trophies on my shelf.

Just let there be some time for me,

to heal and let my life be free:

From darker thoughts that still appear.

From times I rather not be here.

From moments that invade my calm.

From things that seek to cause alarm.

From battles I am scared to fight.

From restless days and sleepless nights.

From doubts I have about my worth.

If only wishes could be heard.

But who knows, maybe one day soon,

when we can go beyond the moon,

I'll be much closer to that star,

and he might say, "Ah, there you are!"

He'd ask me what my wish would be,

what would I have him do for me?

Then I'd reply in just one breath:

Please let me live before my death.

***

Madame Moon

Tonight, you took my breath away,

a perfect view to end my day.

From your face a silver glow,

to light Skiathos town below.

I'm forced to stop within my tracks,

and watch this gem that's set in black.

I wished that I could reach up high,

to pluck its lustre from the sky.

Why have so many writ of you.

in song, in rhyme, a verse or two?

Is it your beauty in our sight,

that makes us so compelled to write?

You paint a true romantic sky,

yet in your beams the wolves do cry.

And many folks have lost their minds,

beneath your full celestial shine.

What is this voodoo you possess,

that steals my gaze at your behest?

What magic does beguile me so,

that I am loath to watch you go?

Then clouds drift by to mask your glare,

breaking my hypnotic stare.

I smile and tip my hat to you,

for moments spent within your hue.

But though you faded for a while,

I shrugged and spared a knowing smile.

For just like Vera's wartime croon:

We'll meet again ... dear Madame Moon.

****

Night Garden

Nightfall sweeps across the sky,

the day has past once more.

I listen to the creatures stir,

outside my own front door.

I sit and gaze at silhouettes,

of hills that loom afar.

Their black shrouds pinpricked here and there,

as house lights mimic stars.

A lone dog barks across the town

and shakes me from my muse.

A breeze arrives with cooling breath,

and rustles through the leaves.

I sense that something's watching me,

so close, yet out of sight.

A cat? A mouse? A snake perhaps?

A mystery of the night.

Yet I don't fear whatever lurks,

it will not do me harm.

Just curious of what it sees:

some stranger in the dark.

The scent of basil in the air,

a sweet and fragrant herb.

A nightingale takes up the stage,

to sing a calming verse.

Shaped like onyx arrow heads,

I watch the Bats flit by.

Such a polished air display,

by creatures that are blind.

I never thought I'd find a way,

to lessen all my woes.

But this could be the remedy,

and hope within me grows.

No need to wander as a cloud,

nor float o'er vale and hill.

I'll sit within my night garden,

my solitary thrill.

Lullaby Rain

Like the swell of acclaim in a great concert hall,

my roof tiles resound as the rain starts to fall.

A crescendo of notes from its rapturous beat,

mystically soothing, contrarily bleak.

I'm drawn to the sound, like a cobra to flute.

Mesmerised, hypnotised, my senses transmute.

Once focused and energised, ready to roll,

my eyelids now laden and desperate to close.

But how does such comfort from deluge appear?

This product of nature not often revered.

Perhaps it's because I'm content where I lay,

allowing the rhythm to steal me away.

I care not to venture outside in the pour,

feeling those pellets of cold chill my bones.

So here in my bed is the place I will stay,

and let the rain lull me, if just for today.

But then, like the curtains that close on a play;

when euphoric encores have faded away.

The rainfall turns mute as it exits stage left,

leaving my feeling of comfort bereft.

Yet this is November and one thing's for sure,

the rain will return to beguile me once more.

Reciting the lines that I've heard time again:

that bitter sweet sonnet of Lullaby Rain.

***

A change of mind

The other day was full of glee,

I even dressed my Xmas tree.

Gazed upon it for a while,

as memories grew to make me smile.

I know I went to sleep that night,

happy and content with life.

Presumed I'd feel the same next day,

but, depression doesn't work that way.

I woke to pangs of lethargy,

its roots gripped deep inside of me.

Making me forgo the right,

to live the day with some delight.

I dwelled on all the negative,

feeling guilty that I lived,

when people worth much more than me,

had lost their lives so tragically.

The day felt dark and winter tide,

despite the sun that shone outside.

And though the sky was perfect blue,

I only saw a dismal hue.

This change in me just makes no sense;

this sudden shift in temperament.

I really wish I could explain,

why all at once I'm down again.

I'm blessed to have a decent life.

I do not starve nor face real strife.

So why, do I feel such distress

and caged inside an emptiness?

I don't invite, I do not crave,

the tears that fall without my say.

But ask me why I'm weeping so?

I couldn't say, I just don't know.

It isn't one thing, isn't two,

it's ALL the bad thoughts seeping through.

As if a filter in my mind,

the one that's labelled "rationalise",

has broken down, its fuses blown,

allowing all this crap to flow.

And so I turn my hand to rhyme,

cathartic words to ease my mind.

To find perspective, help me see,

that there are some worse off than me.

But more than that, I need to share,

with all likeminded souls out there,

that if you feel all hope has gone

and have no will to carry on,

then reach out, call out, shout it loud,

don't sit in pain beneath that cloud.

No pride should come before a fall.

Don't feel ashamed, impart it all.

Just take my lead and let it go.

Believe me, you are NOT alone.

***

The stranger

There once was a stranger dressed wholly in black,

who mixed with the poor and the aristocrats.

He hadn't a penny and ne'er owned a lot,

but nevertheless, he shared what he'd got.

He travelled the world and mingled with folk,

yet some just ignored him and called him a joke.

But he wasn't fazed by their ignorant deeds,

nor was he biased to colour or creed.

His single objective was changing the world.

To preach to the people and make himself heard.

But this he would do without making a scene,

then gather his flock by unsavoury means.

His name is mnemonic, in literal terms.

His full title wasn't the one we would learn.

And we speak of him boldly, yet silently plead:

Oh Lord, please protect me from Covid Nineteen.

***

When?

A poem of realisation

When did I decide to swap my nights out for the telly?

When was it acceptable to carry such a belly?

When did I begin to crave my pjs and my slippers?

When did it become the time to purchase nasal clippers?

When did I ... like ever …care about my constitution?

Now I'm eating prunes to help resolve a lack of movement.

When did I begin to tire so far before eleven?

When did peace and quiet turn into my idea of heaven?

When did I decide to tune my radio to Smooth?

And what's with all that chart filled noise they try to pass as groove?

Hip-hop-rap-crap, garage, grunge,

all sounds to drive me mad.

Oh when, oh when, dear Lord above,

did I turn into my dad?

When did the kids, that I saw born, get children of their own?

When did I start to talk to me, whilst bumbling around my home?

When did all my body parts, begin to creak and moan?

When did simply standing up, not pass without a groan?

New spectacles, old testicles, the latter on decline.

Pills for this and sprays for that, to keep me feeling fine.

Mirrors show a different me, to the image in my mind.

I can't deny - nor can I hide - those bags beneath my eyes .

My hair - or should I say what's left of it - is slowly turning grey.

My eyes are dim, my skin less taut, I'm pissing more each day.

If I could only turn back time, reset the youthful clock.

But would I change the life I've lived? No ... probably not.

So, here's the thing.

Despite the fact I'm getting old, despite these ageing signs.

I'll seize the day as best I can, until it's time to die.

For looks and age won't mean a thing, when lying in that box.

So, I'll resolve to love my life, before the reaper knocks.

May I suggest you do the same?

***

An ode to tea

I have to say - you might agree -

there's nothing like a cup of tea.

It helps you face the day ahead

and soothes you when it's time for bed.

A splash of milk, if that's your need.

Dunk a biscuit, read the leaves.

Make a pot or just a cup.

Someone boil the kettle up.

So many flavours now to choose,

from peppermint to ginger root.

Different blends, the latest fad,

though I prefer a Tetley's bag.

Just one contains a zillion holes,

to help the flavour's slow unroll.

Yet whilst this is my go-to blend,

it isn't where the char list ends … oh no my friends.

Black tea, white tea, copper top.

Sugar laced, to help with shock.

Loose leaf, decaf, added spice.

Lipton's lemon, freshly iced.

A rather British way of life,

to have a brew amidst our strife.

How else would all our troubles flee,

without the help of Rosy Lee?

The drink of choice for kings and queens,

a beverage that is quite supreme.

As Austen said - that's Jane, not Steve:

"I'd rather having nothing but tea!"

And so I'll end with just one plea.

Go fill your mugs with good old tea.

Then raise your cups and spread the news.

There's nothing like a well-made brew.

***

Deceit

"Come on in, my fine young friend,"

said the spider to the fly.

"I wish to show you magic that will fascinate your mind."

"I'm not supposed to be near you,"

the fly buzzed in reply.

"My father told me of your sort and warned me not to pry!"

"I know of whom your father speaks,"

said spider with a sigh.

"But I'm an old arachnid. I will not do you harm."

He shrugged and turned himself away.

The fly, he pondered deep.

"I'm sure it wouldn't hurt at all, to take a little peep."

"So, what's your magic trick about?"

The fly called out with zest.

The spider fixed a saddened look, then turned to face his guest.

"It matters not my curious chap,"

he uttered with dismay.

"Your father's words mean so much more than magic tricks today."

The fly took one step closer,

his tone became quite stern.

"I'll do just what I want to do. How else am I to learn!"

The spider gave a thrilled exclaim

and beckoned to the fly.

"Then step inside my magic house, the show's about to start."

The fly walked in, the spider grinned,

Then set upon his prey.

He couldn't help but laugh out loud.

"Another fool today!"

The fly looked scared, he couldn't move,

his legs were stuck like glue.

His wings flapped hard, to no avail,

there was nothing he could do.

He watched the spider bare his fangs,

then felt him take a bite.

And as the venom seeped inside,

he lost the will to fight.

And though his life was fading fast,

he heard his father scold.

"I warned you of the dangers son, why wouldn't you be told?"

The moral of this poem's words

are simple in their form.

Listen well to good advice, before you take a fall.

It isn't hard to comprehend,

just yearn to live, not die.

For Covid is the spider's name, so please … don't be the fly.

***

How long?

How many times do I have to say?

"I'm pretty good, I feel okay."

The same reply each time I'm asked,

but how long must I wear this mask?

The one you see from day to day,

smiling, joking, lots to say.

A great disguise that's just for you,

hiding what I'm going through.

How many times do I have to lie,

that I'm just great, I'm getting by?

When what I really need to say,

is "Fuck, this an awful day!"

But of this cloud I will not speak,

for fear that people think I'm weak.

Silent doubts of what I feel,

if it can't be seen, it can't be real … right?

So, I will stay behind this mask,

and try to bring my mind to task.

I'll keep on asking every day,

how long must I be trapped this way?

Though someday soon I hope to find,

solutions for my peace of mind,

I fear I seek what ne'er can be?

Oh Lord, how long till I am back to me?

***

Grounded - A teenager's reaction.

I'm worn, I'm torn, I wish I wasn't born.

I'm mad, I'm sad, I'm treated oh so bad.

Not fair. Don't care. You wish I wasn't there.

You've been, so mean. You know that I'm fourteen … right?

Mum moaned. Dad groaned. And then they took my phone.

Now doom, and gloom, they've sent me to my room.

Whatever. I'll never, speak to them, like ever.

So cruel. Not cool. It's worse than being at school.

So bare, unfair. I'll stomp on up the stairs.

Then whine, that line: "I'm phoning Child Line!"

"Okay," they say. "Good luck with that today!"

"I'll leave!" I seethe. A threat they don't believe.

In bed, I said: "At least you love me, Ted."

I cried, then sighed: "They ground me all the time!"

I shrug, then hug, my quilt until I'm snug.

Don't mind. I'm fine. I think I'll close my eyes.

Count sheep, to sleep, I will not make a peep.

Count sheep, to sleep …

Night Ted.

***

Tomorrow Never Came

I'm here before you, lost for words,

not knowing what to say.

I didn't think I'd see you soon,

I didn't plan this day.

I'm not sure what I'm feeling now,

or how I should react.

But here I stand in front of you

and know I can't go back.

Am I supposed to show remorse,

for every wrong I've done?

Or thank you for the gift of life,

despite the fact it's gone?

And though your lips don't move at all,

I hear all what you say.

You ask me if I made my mark

or merely breathed each day?

On that I cannot answer true,

yet let this truth be heard.

I tried to be a righteous man,

I tried to show my worth.

But only those I've left behind

can judge the life I've led.

Will I be praised? Will I be damned?

The latter's what I dread.

But here I stand in front of you,

wishing that I'd tried,

to fill my life with all the gifts,

you'd placed before my eyes.

I wish I'd travelled far and wide,

I wish I'd learnt to dance.

I wish I'd done so many things,

but now I've lost the chance.

For just like many in the world,

I squandered every breath.

And put on hold my bucket list,

not contemplating death.

So now I'll drown in retrospect,

of pleasures never claimed.

I filled all my "tomorrows",

but tomorrow never came.

And though I've come to realise,

it's much too late for me,

I'll make myself your conscious guide,

and tell you what will be.

That life is not to be rehearsed,

so live it come what may.

Your time on Earth is precious friends,

don't fritter it away.

You only get one crack at this,

there is no second half.

So, before you're up here next to me,

be sure to leave your mark.

***